THIS BOOK IS

......David Butler

THE WORLD'S MOST DELIGHTFUL/ UGLY/CHARMING/SEXY/CRUDE/ BORING/CUTE/STUPID/CANCERIAN

BEST WISHES FROM/YOURS IN DISGUST ALL MY LOVE ...Vera...............

P.S. PLEASE TAKE NOTE OF PAGE(S)

..34, 45, 5, 7, 10.....................

THE CANCER BOOK

A CORGI BOOK 0 552 12319 6

First publication in Great Britain
PRINTING HISTORY
Corgi edition published 1983
Corgi edition reissued 1984

Corgi Books are published by Transworld Publishers Ltd., Century House, 61-63 Uxbridge Road, Ealing, London W5 5SA.

Made and printed in Great Britain by the Guernsey Press Co. Ltd., Guernsey, Channel Islands.

THE CANCER BOOK

BY IAN HEATH

CANCER

JUNE 21 – JULY 20

FOURTH SIGN OF THE ZODIAC

SYMBOL : THE CRAB

RULING PLANET : THE MOON

COLOURS : WHITE, SEA-GREEN

GEMS : PEARL, AQUAMARINE

NUMBER : TWO

DAY : MONDAY

METAL : SILVER

FLOWER : MAGNOLIA

zzzzzzzzzzzzzz
The
CANCERIAN
at work.................

.....KNOWS HIS/HER VALUE..........

......IS PIG-HEADED..............

... CLIMBS TO TOP OF THE LADDER ....

....CAN BE OLD-FASHIONED........

......IS A WORRIER.....................

....KNOWS WHAT PEOPLE WANT.....

.....IS GOOD AT FIGURES.........

.... FAIRLY AGGRESSIVE ....

RATHER SHY

......AND DOESN'T PANIC.

VACANCIES

The CANCERIAN finds success as...

......AN ARCHAEOLOGIST............

..... RIDING INSTRUCTOR ....

......SHIP'S CAPTAIN..................

........GARDENER.......................

..........WAITRESS.......................

...MARRIAGE COUNSELLOR.........

.... OR BANK-MANAGER.

The
CANCERIAN
at home

........IS A HOARDER ....

.......LIKES TO BE WARM..........

.......IS VIDEO—CRAZY...............

.........ABSENT-MINDED..............

VERY STRICT

....ENJOYS WALKING THE DOG........

WINE-MAKING

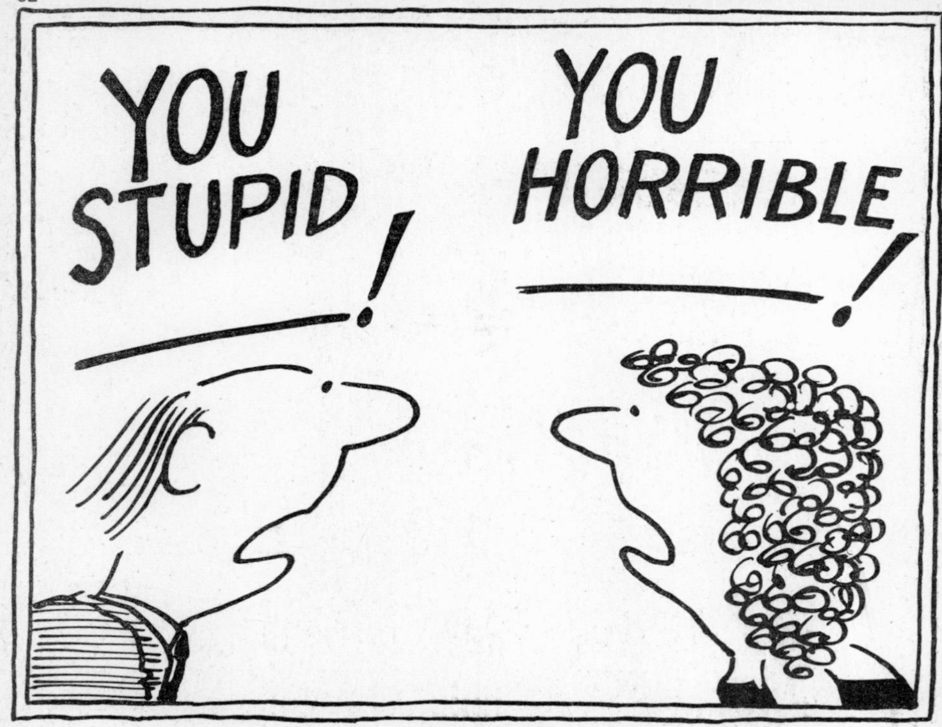

.......LOVES WORD GAMES.........

........READING LONG NOVELS..........

.....AND LIKES SILENCE.

The
CANCERIAN
likes..............

........BALLROOM DANCING........

FAST CARS

......COLLECTING BUTTERFLIES........

........HORSE–RIDING...............

BUBBLE-BATHS

... AND BUBBLE-GUM.

The CANCERIAN dislikes ....

SNAKES

SOAP-OPERAS

……NOISY CHILDREN…………

......INCOME TAX DEMANDS.........

.........KEEPING FIT.................

......AND GARLIC.

The CANCERIAN in love . . . .

.....HAS HIGH STANDARDS........

... DOESN'T LIKE MAKE-UP.........

..... WON'T LET GO..................

.... IS TENDER ....

.....CAN BE TEARFUL...............

......CONCEALS PASSION..........

........LAUGHS A LOT..............

.....IS YOUNG-AT-HEART............

...HAS TO TELL THE WORLD..........

.... AND IS SHY.

CANCERIAN AND PARTNER

HEART RATINGS

♥♥♥♥♥ WOWEE !!

♥♥♥♥ GREAT, BUT NOT 'IT'

♥♥♥ O.K.— COULD BE FUN

♥♥ FORGET IT

♥ WALK QUICKLY THE OTHER WAY

SCORPIO PISCES

LEO VIRGO GEMINI
TAURUS

ARIES CANCER

LIBRA CAPRICORN

SAGITTARIUS AQUARIUS

CANCER PEOPLE

GEORGE ORWELL : HENRY VIII
REMBRANDT : LOUIS ARMSTRONG
JULIUS CAESER : JEAN COCTEAU
INGMAR BERGMAN : NEIL SIMON
RINGO STARR : THE DUKE OF WINDSOR

YUL BRYNNER : JAMES CAGNEY
OLIVIA DE HAVILLAND
GINGER ROGERS : MARCEL PROUST
JOHN GLENN : GINA LOLLOBRIGIDA
OSCAR HAMMERSTEIN II
DAVID HOCKNEY : ADAM FAITH
DIANA, PRINCESS OF WALES
HAMMOND INNES : DIANA RIGG
SIR LEONARD HUTTON
IRIS MURDOCH : ILIE NASTASE
SIR EDMUND HILLARY
GEORGIE FAME : VIRGINIA WADE